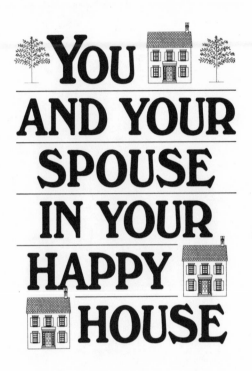

YOU AND YOUR SPOUSE IN YOUR HAPPY HOUSE

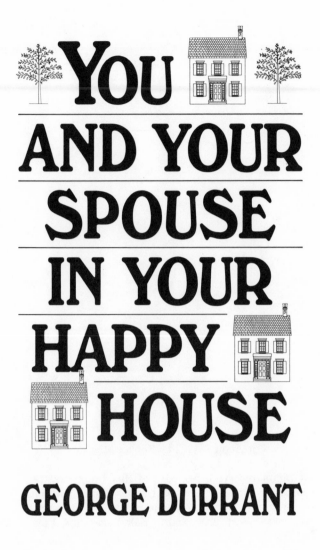

YOU AND YOUR SPOUSE IN YOUR HAPPY HOUSE

GEORGE DURRANT

Bookcraft
Salt Lake City, Utah

Library of Congress Catalog Card Number: 92-72665
ISBN 0-88494-844-7

Second Printing, 1993

Printed in the United States of America

The house in which we
live will have but
little to do with our
happiness.

But the spouse with
whom we live will
have almost
everything
to do with our
happiness.

This book is dedicated to
Marilyn,
who has made
me happier
than
I
could have
ever
dreamed.

Best of Luck.
Always stay close to the
spirit — Weber State University 8th Word
Bishop

Contents

1

Your First Little House

They tore it down.

I can't believe they actually tore it down.

They tore it down and built a condominium.

Didn't they know what it was?

Did they leave any room to build a monument to commemorate what happened there?

Oh, I agree it didn't look like much. The house was old, and the apartment that had been built on the back had the appearance of a tar-paper shack. The value wasn't in the lumber, the bricks, or the shingles; rather, it was what happened under the shingles, above the floors, and between the walls that made it sacred.

But they didn't know, so they tore it down.

I forgive them. Maybe someday when I'm rich, I'll

buy a few feet on the corner of the lot and build a monument myself. I'll build it out of cream-colored bricks, and I'll attach a brass plaque with these words engraved:

On this lot there once stood an old house, attached to the back of which was a very small apartment. In 1956, from January to August, that small apartment was the first home of the newly married couple George and Marilyn Durrant. This monument commemorates the happiness that each of them had in this, their first little house.

Ah yes! Our first little house. The kitchen swept into the front room, which opened into the bedroom. Actually it was a sort of triple combination—three rooms in one. We couldn't afford chairs, so we sat on our suitcases. We had learned to sit on them during the last days of our missions.

We didn't have much in the way of material things—very little furniture, no car, and rather meager amounts of food. But, oh my! We sure were happy!

Our joy came from our love. Little things keyed our feelings, things like this sentiment expressed by a profound poet describing a newly married couple's deepest emotions:

She looked at him, and her heart
was all aflutter.
He had just written "I love you"
in the butter.

Maybe if they had known all that had happened in that little house, they would not have torn it down. But then again, maybe they did know. Perhaps they knew that houses are not happiness; instead, they are places, be they large or small, where happiness happens. Though houses may come and go, the happy memories that are made in them can never be torn down or taken away. And the only monuments to love and happiness that matter are the ones built in our hearts.

So I have no animosity towards those who tore it down, for it will stand as a treasured memory forever—our first little house.

Since that first house, we have moved on. First to an upstairs apartment near Fort Chaffee, Arkansas; then to a "duplex," part of which was in Korea, where I lived, the other part of which was in Provo, Utah, seven thousand miles away where Marilyn lived. Next came our apartment in the David John men's residence hall at Brigham Young University, where we supervised 260 young men. Then to the first house that we actually owned, which was located in beautiful Brigham City, Utah. Next we returned to one, then two, then three houses in Provo. After that, we moved on to the two-story gray house in Salt Lake City. From there to the spacious mission home in Louisville, Kentucky, and then back to the white lumber house in Provo. Next was the house in Mt. Olympus Cove, with a view of the entire Salt Lake Valley. Finally, we came back to the house in Provo.

Right about now you might be thinking to yourself, "George and Marilyn sure did live in a lot of different houses."

To that I reply, "Well, I'm not sure about that. We just seemed to take the space that filled the rooms from one house to another. For us, our home was always independent from our houses. Home was the place I always longed to be. Home was where Marilyn was. Home was where the children were. Whenever I was away, my heart always refused to travel with me, and it always stayed home. So, I'll acknowledge that we did have several houses, but we had only one home."

When Marilyn and I decided to get married, I thought no one had ever been so in love. I was sure that our love could never be deeper than it was on the day we were wed and during our time in our first house. But now I know that the love we felt in those early days was really but a starter kit that ignited a more permanent flame, a flame that burns so much brighter now than I ever thought possible back then.

Elizabeth Eamons described my feeling with these words:

> When love and I are met,
> I used to say,
> I shall be certain from the first hello—
> No wondering about it, no delay.
> I thought a steady flame in us would glow
> As if we lit a candle each in each.
> But in my ignorance I did not know nor
>   understand
> That love's coming may be slow.
> I didn't know that love, if it be true,
> May need a thousand greetings
> While it sends its roots so deep
> That neither of the two hearts can be freed.
> I didn't know that friends as
> Dear as you and I were in the past
> Could take the gates of paradise at last.

In our thirteen thousand days together, Marilyn

and I have exchanged much more than "a thousand greetings." Inside our little houses we have passed through some difficult pains and have felt the joy of a multitude of quiet pleasures. The roots of our love have indeed grown so deep "that neither of [our] two hearts can be freed."

The longer we live together, the further we seem to pass through and even beyond the gates of paradise and into heaven itself.

I'm not saying that our marriage has been perfect, but I am saying it has been wonderful. In this book, I'll point out a few of the things that have helped make it so. I hope the ideas herein will be helpful to those of you who are now married and also to those who dream of the day when you and your future spouse will live together in love in your little house.

Yes, they tore it down—our first little house. Perhaps I won't build the cream-colored brick monument to our first house, because that would not be fair to our other houses. So I'll let that idea go. Instead, I'll just keep adding bricks of joy to the monument that occupies the dearest part of my heart, the portion of my heart that has a sign on the door which reads, "Only family members are authorized to enter and forever remain herein." Perhaps it is that portion of our hearts where home really is.

2

Wondering About Your Future Spouse and Your Future House

Sometimes, when a young fellow is in high school, if he is really handsome, the Lord causes him to be timid so that he won't get too involved with girls. I was really timid. Perhaps that is the Lord's way of protecting young men from the girls and from getting too involved with romance at too early an age.

Be that true or not, the girls in my high school were quite willing to let me graduate without much romantic involvement. But that didn't stop me from wondering if I'd ever have a girlfriend, or if I'd ever fall in love and have someone fall in love with me. I wondered if I'd ever get married, and if so, I wondered who she'd be.

Such thoughts didn't consume all of my thinking time, because I had to spend 2 or 3 percent of my thinking power in school. And sports—especially basketball—required about 87 percent of my thoughts. That seemed right because at that time in my life basketball was a lot more important than marriage. However, once in a while, especially after the March tournaments had all been played and the warm weather of April brought the green grass and the cherry blossoms to our valley, I'd wonder just a little about romance.

Finally, I was of missionary age. I had just purchased a navy blue suit, and I felt that I looked quite good in it. I thought to myself, "The best use I could make of such a suit is to go on a mission." Not long after that, I had my call. I'll always remember my farewell. Because our new ward meetinghouse was just being built, our meetings were held in the seminary building just off the hill from the old American Fork high school. The room where we held sacrament meeting was quite small, which made the crowd that came to my farewell seem enormous. And what really added to the numbers was the throng of girls who attended. I mean, there were girls from as far away as Springville, nearly twenty miles distant.

After the meeting, as I shook hands with each young lady, I sensed that they seemed to like me. I wondered why I hadn't discovered that before. I sort of attributed their feelings to the way I looked in the navy blue suit, but I'm sure that it was more than that.

That night as I retired to my bed, I wondered about the future: First I wondered about my mission and how that would go. Then I wondered about, well, about the girls at my farewell and girls in general—and about one unknown girl in particular. I wondered about life, and marriage, and children.

After quite some time, I had wondered about almost every glorious thing there is to wonder about. Finally, I became weary, and I silently prayed myself to sleep.

What about you? Did you used to wonder about your future? Did you dream while you were wide awake about who might someday be your spouse? Did you wonder when your dream would unfold? Now, looking back, has your dream come true? Have things worked out the way you dreamed? I hope so, but you and I both know that sometimes things go wrong. To you who have had your dreams shattered, I say, "Hang on. Dream more dreams, and someday, somehow, all will be well."

To you who are happily married and who have been in such bliss for months or years or decades—perhaps more than half a century—I ask, "What is the secret to marital happiness?" As you read this book, compare the feelings that I express with your own. See how closely you feel that I come to the truths that you know.

To you younger ones whose next chapter or two of life will bring you closer to marriage, I say, "I wish you well." I pray that, when the time comes, you young men will have the desire and the strength to move forward into marriage. For you young women who hope to marry a noble man, I pray that someday he will come along and that he will be strong. Until he comes along, remember that although you need not marry in this life to have eternal joy, you must always *desire* to be married if the right and willing one comes along. All of us know that love approaches at surprising times and from unsuspecting directions. Keep your eyes and your hearts open and be ready.

3

Finding and Choosing Your Spouse

For some of you at an earlier time and for others of you now or hopefully in the near future, the major question of life is, "Who will be the spouse that will live with me in my little house?"

Through the years I have often met young people who were striving to find an answer to that vital question. They ask themselves, "How will I know if I am really in love? How will I know if this one is indeed the right one?"

From those with such wondering awe, I have also heard comments such as these: "I'm certain that I've found the right one, but the right one for me is not certain that I'm the right one. I've prayed, and I feel the Lord is saying, 'Yes, go ahead,' but my sweetheart feels the Lord has said, 'No, go back.' Why do we get different answers?"

I used to feel that all people fell in love "head over heels." After all, that was what happened to me. But after talking to many others, I've found that such sweeping and breathtaking love does not readily come to some. Some seem not to really fall in love at all. Rather, they just sort of cautiously slip into a state of not quite being able to go forward to marriage nor back to satisfied singleness. While many are at one of these two extremes—head over heels in love or uncomfortably uncertain—others may be somewhere in between.

The following fictitious story expresses some basic truths about choosing a spouse and living happily thereafter in your little house. I've titled the story "The Decision."

The Decision

Hello, my name is Gary. After serving a mission, I decided to keep looking for a golden contact. You know—someone who deserves the very best, someone who would be my spouse. I was in no great hurry to marry, yet at the same time I felt that I was somehow marching in place in my overall life. I considered myself to be like a Latter-day Saint who had departed from Nauvoo and crossed the Mississippi River but was now camped on the western shore and wasn't headed west to the promised land. So, I kept my eyes open for someone who wanted to go west with me.

Soon I was well acquainted with three young

ladies, each of whom had caught my fancy. Their names were Betty, Susan, and Zetta. As the weeks passed by, I became more enamored of Betty, but I just wasn't sure if she was really the one. Oh, yes, she met all the qualifications I'd dreamed of in a wife, and she was deeply committed to the gospel. But the decision loomed large.

To know for a certainty what I should do, I made it a matter of fervent prayer. I knelt in a private place and asked the Lord, "Should I marry Betty?" Still on my knees, I waited and waited for the answer, but I didn't hear or even feel an answer. Finally I decided that the answer must be yes. The next evening, while Betty and I walked under the stars, I mustered up all my courage and asked her to marry me.

She gently and kindly replied, "Oh, Gary, you are so wonderful, and I like you a lot. But I am waiting for Charles."

So I had prayed to know if I should marry Betty, and now in a very real way the Lord had answered my prayer. The answer to my question, "Should I marry Betty?" was no.

A few days later, I was walking north toward the Marriott Center on the BYU campus to attend a devotional assembly. Suddenly I heard someone call out my name. I looked to my right, and there sitting on the lawn in the sunshine I saw Zetta. She beckoned me to come over.

As I walked toward her, she asked, "Where are you going in such a hurry?"

"To the devotional," I replied in an enthusiastic tone.

I was a little shocked when she replied, "Don't go there. It's too pretty a day to be inside. Sit here by me under this tree."

When I heard her invitation, I had to admit to myself that it was indeed a pretty day. I felt a bit flattered that she had called me to come to join her, because she was the prettiest girl on campus.

Sort of reluctantly, but kind of willingly, I agreed to sit with her. It certainly wouldn't hurt my image to have all the passersby see me with her. My only regret was that I felt I needed the strength that I knew I would receive from the devotional talk.

But my regret was soon swallowed up in the fun and excitement of exchanging words and laughs with one so charming as Zetta.

Finally, it was time for her and me to go to our noon classes. It was hard for me to leave her, and I sensed that she felt the same about leaving me. We quickly agreed to a Friday night date, and as I walked away I felt my heart pounding within my chest. To myself I said, "Hey! This might be the one."

In the weeks that followed, Zetta and I had some heart-to-heart talks. She liked many of the same things that I did, but I began to notice some differences—some major differences. Zetta didn't share the spiritual values that were so dear to me. She liked the gospel, but she didn't see it as being at the center of her happiness. I sensed that she . . . well, I just wasn't sure.

That night I prayed for direction in making my decision. I asked the Lord, "Should I pursue this, and if Zetta is willing, should I marry her?"

This time as I paused to await an answer, I was more certain that I did hear a voice. It was a quiet voice, or perhaps it was an inward idea. At any rate, I felt a certain no. Try as I would, because I really liked her, I could not continue to pursue a course that would lead to our marriage.

So that left Susan. After Zetta and I had gone our

separate ways, Susan and I began to date quite often. She seemed to bring out the best in me. I'm not always the strongest guy in the world, but I have an intense desire to do the right thing. Susan helped me do so, and I guess I did the same for her.

I can't say that I was madly in love with her, but I sure respected her and I loved being with her. I felt comfortable and peaceful when I was with her. When we were separated for a day, or once for a week, I longed to be with her.

I could tell that she really liked me. As a matter of fact, she told me so. I slowly began to wonder about having her as my spouse. Each day that idea seemed better.

Of course, I had done some preliminary praying about our relationship, but now, after three months of close association, it was time to do some "main event" praying.

On my knees, I asked, "Should I marry Susan?" I waited and waited. All I could hear was a long, profound silence. There had not been a no, but, on the other hand, there had not been any yes.

The next day was Friday, and Susan and I were going to make tacos in her apartment for dinner. We did so and then decided to go to a carnival that was in town. When I saw the huge Ferris wheel, an idea came into my head that sent a smile across my face from one ear to the other.

At the top of the ride, I took Susan by the hand and said, "Susan, I feel I could go to the top of the world with you, and that we could go round and round forever. Will you marry me, Susan? If you say yes, I'll get you a ring as big as this Ferris wheel."

I'll have to admit it was frightening to be up so high with someone as excited as she was. I thought she might upset our bench and dump us both out.

She clung to me, and over and over again shouted, "Yes! Yes! Yes!"

As we got off, I asked, "Don't you want to pray about it to see if it's right?" She faced me and held both of my hands. "Pray about it! I've prayed all my teenage years for someone like you. I don't need to ask Heavenly Father if it's okay. All he has wanted me to do is find someone who loves him as much as I do and someone I love as much as I love you. Then he wants me to tell him who I chose to marry, so he can share in my excitement." With that, she shouted "I love you, Gary!" so loud that several people turned and stared. Taking my hand and pulling me through the crowd, she excitedly said, "Let's go home. I want to phone Daddy and tell him."

A week or so later, Susan and I walked up on the mountain that overlooks the Provo Temple. We could see the Missionary Training Center that was nearby. That brought back a multitude of memories.

Then, while holding hands on the mountainside, we talked of our upcoming temple marriage. Standing and looking over the valley, we prayed. "Oh, dear Heavenly Father, we thank thee that we have been guided in our lives by the truths of thy gospel. We are grateful that we have found each other and that thou hast answered our lifelong prayers.

"We present ourselves to you and announce to you our marriage plans. Thou art cordially invited to attend our temple marriage and to be part of our lives forever. We thank thee that thou hast allowed us to choose for ourselves to marry each other. Now that, with thy help, we have made this decision, we humbly ask thee to do for us that which thou didst for the stones which the brother of Jared presented to you. Please reach down and touch our lives so that our lives will, like those stones, light up. Bless us that we will have children and that we will live thy ways and teach our children to do the same. Give us light as thou didst give light unto the Jaredites. Reach down from heaven and touch us so that we will be the happiest family that there could ever be."

When we said amen, we heard the Lord speak to us in our hearts. He said, "I will touch you. Yes, I will."

So the story of Gary and Susan and their decision comes to a conclusion—or to a beginning.

It is my feeling that in most cases the Lord has given us a standard to judge who would or would not be a suitable spouse for us. When we find such a person, and when we sense that we are in first-degree, or even third-degree, love with him or her, then we should proceed. The Lord is ready to touch you and your sweetheart, your spouse. And as you and your spouse live in harmony with Heavenly Father's plan in your little house, He will indeed touch you and your family so that you will light up, so that you will always have light and see into heaven while living on earth, and so that you will always know the joy of the Lord.

4

Loving Your Spouse in Your Little House

The Humber River that flows through Yorkshire, England, and empties into the North Sea would never be named on a travel guide's list of the top ten most beautiful rivers in the world. But on my list, it is number one. "Why," you ask, "would that be the case?" Let me explain.

In 1955 I stood on a dock that runs parallel to the flow of the murky brown waters of the Humber. At my back was the great city of Kingston Upon Hull, commonly known as Hull. Hull, England. I'd never even heard the name of that city before my mission. But after my orientation in London, my mission president, A. Hamer Reiser, looked into my eyes and said, "Elder Durrant, you go to Hull."

Sensing that I was a bit startled, he chuckled and

said, "Not the place opposite of heaven, but Hull, Yorkshire, England." I was relieved at his clarification, and an hour later I was on the train headed for Hull. Little did I know then that Hull, England, would become for me "Heaven," England.

I spent my entire mission in Hull. Here I loved and was loved in return. Here the foundation of my whole life was laid. Here I taught and was taught the glorious gospel of Jesus Christ. Here I came to know that the heavens had again been opened and that God and Christ had appeared to restore all truth. Here I truly found my pearl of great price.

So now as I stood with both Hull and nearly all my mission behind me, I was filled with deep, inexpressible joy.

At my side stood a man who, to me, represented all that I had come to treasure. He was then one of the Twelve Apostles of the Lord. He and I stood apart from a group of twenty or so who would soon catch the ferryboat that would cross the Humber to New Holland. There we'd catch a train for Grimsby and have a special conference.

Since the ferry would not be ready for us to board for nearly an hour or so, there was time to talk.

Being on the dock with this loving leader caused me to feel that I almost stood there with the Savior himself. I had never felt such joy. As we looked out at the slowly moving current, the leader said many things to me about living water and the waters of baptism. After concluding those thoughts, he paused and asked, looking into my eyes, "Elder Durrant, how do you feel about yourself and your mission?"

I tried to express just how dear my mission was to me.

He then asked, "Do you have any special concerns that you would like to discuss with me?"

I stood for several seconds silently gazing across nearly a mile at the distant shore. Then I spoke, "There is one concern."

He and I both waited for the other to say more. Finally, I continued, "There is a sister missionary serving in our district. She has been here her entire mission, as have I. I have seen her often. She now serves in Scarborough. She has brought many to the truth, enough for an entire branch of the Church. I have seen her teach, and I've felt the power of her testimony."

I paused, and we both watched a motorboat making its way against the modest current.

I continued, "I have such great respect for her. I really feel I love her."

I said no more. He spoke by asking, "Is it Sister Burnham?"

I looked into his eyes and answered softly, "Yes, it is."

He smiled and replied, "I don't blame you for feeling as you do. I just interviewed her, and she is impressive."

I smiled and nodded my head in agreement.

He reached forward and held the rail with both hands as he began to tell me things I shall never forget:

"Elder Durrant, you have fallen in love spiritually. That's all you can do on a mission. But that is not enough to allow you to know what the future will bring. So now you must put this matter aside until your mission is concluded.

"Then when you return home, you can determine if you not only love her spiritually but also physically. Because, you see, love must be both of those ways, both spiritual and physical. Neither the physical side of love and marriage nor the spiritual side can be complete without the other."

The ferry's whistle beckoned us aboard. The hour had passed, and my powerful and life-guiding lesson was over.

Our mission president and I talked as we crossed the Humber. I recounted the experience I had just had and suggested a transfer for either Sister Burnham or myself. He looked deep into my eyes and said, "I won't transfer either of you, because I trust you." He added, "Elder Durrant, to be trusted is a greater compliment than to be loved."

A month later, Sister Burnham—whose first name, I later learned, was Marilyn—finished her greatly successful mission and returned home. Four months later, I did also.

As the domeliner train made the final leg of its journey from New York to Utah, it wound its way through the Colorado Rockies. I sat in silence considering the future. Two hours later, the train slowed and then stopped at the Provo, Utah, station. I was home.

As I climbed down the two stairs to the platform, I saw my mother. I took her in my arms and felt inexpressible joy, love, and gratitude. Because of her teachings and her profound sacrifices, I had found my own soul.

After greeting other family members, I saw Sister Burnham. My heart leaped within me. Seeing that I had greeted all the others, she walked to me and we shook hands in a most electrifying manner.

A few days later, I did as the Apostle had counseled. I began gathering information that would help us determine if our love was more than spiritual. We found that it surely was.

Based on the abundance of heartfelt data, on Christmas Eve 1955 I presented to Sister Burnham—by now I called her Marilyn—a small diamond, one of the smallest to ever come out of Africa, but to her it seemed the size of a marble. She quickly accepted my offer.

Because marriage plans take time, we were not married until the following year—January 19, 1956.

The advice I received on the banks of the murky Humber River has been profoundly important to me. The feeling that I felt there and what I learned caused those everflowing waters of the Humber to be the most beautiful of all rivers to me.

And so now to you I say, "'Tis not enough that she is physically beautiful and you are handsome. To that you must add respect, honor, and spiritual depth in order to receive the complete joy of marriage. Nor is it enough that you have great spiritual understanding if physical love is lacking. For then marriage may last, but it won't have the beauty that it could have."

But perhaps these two—physical and spiritual love—are not separate at all but are so overlapping and interwoven that a person cannot discern where one leaves off and the other begins. The answer seems to lie in the Lord's words, "Wherefore, verily I say unto you that all things unto me are spiritual" (D&C 29:34).

I wish I could write more plainly just what I feel. But I think you know what I'm trying to say.

If people knew the value of religion, they would form long lines to get into the chapel. By "religion," I don't mean the outward acts alone. I don't mean just going to church or just partaking of the sacrament. What I mean are the feelings that motivate such acts and the beauty that can and does come as a result. Those motivating feelings make life as different as color television from black and white.

I recall many years ago, our family was watching *The Wizard of Oz* on our black and white TV set. As Dorothy's house flew over the rainbow and was about to crash down in Munchkin Land, I announced to the family, "The story has been in black and white up until this point, but now it will be in color."

Seven-year-old Dwight replied, "Not on our TV set."

"Yeah," I said excitedly, "from now on it will be in color."

"Not on our set," came his certain reply.

"Yeah, on our set," I answered, and as the house came down on the Wicked Witch, I said, "Watch! It will change to color."

"Not on our set," he said with soberness.

As Dorothy investigated Munchkin Land and the Munchkins began to appear, Dwight said in a victorious tone, "See, it is still black and white."

"No, it's in color," I replied.

To try to be correct, I grabbed a box of crayons and tried to color the screen. Munchkins move too fast. You can't color them.

I smiled and said, "Anyway, for me the rest of the story is in color."

In real life, religion can bring living color into our lives. When all things are seen and felt in spiritual light, there comes a beauty that surpasses living color.

So we don't go to church just to be religious there. We go to church and make commitments and feel feelings that will give us the desire and the strength to go home and be religious there too. By "religious," I mean having spiritually uplifting thoughts and desires to be doers of the word, and then indeed doing the things that will lift us and our spouse and our family.

As I write, I feel the power of these ideas. To have spiritual goals; to want to bless the lives of others, especially our family; to kneel in prayer at the bedside with my spouse and then, as a matter of deep love and commitment, to unite in the physical intimacies of marriage—all this is to feel a joy that touches heaven.

Oh, of course, we are not always spiritually in tune, even though we wish with all our hearts that we could be so. We are often pulled down a bit by the opposition of life's challenges. We don't feel very perfect then, do we? But we don't need to be perfect in all things. We just need to wish that we could be, always striving to do the best we can; and we need to say, with a broken heart and a contrite spirit, "Oh, dear God, my spouse and I agree that we are not perfect. But we want you to know that we would be if we could be. And we will do all in our power to live according to your will."

In this attitude, Marilyn and I have felt, as you have felt, that Heavenly Father says, "I understand, and as long as you continue to try, I will bless you with my light and my love."

Two people in this attitude can and will enjoy a physical flame of love that will transcend any problem or challenge and will bring sensitivities that will make life go beyond beautiful. In such a spirit, there can be no holding back, no teasing, no spite. Rather, a perfect giving of physical love will bless you and your spouse with the sweetening and fulfilling influence of spiritual love.

You and your spouse together in love in your little house will be as one, and though a cold blizzard blows outside, it can never chill your hopes, your dreams, and your joy.

Someday, I hope to return to the banks of the Humber and thank Heavenly Father for what I learned there.

5

Children Come to Bless
Your Little House

As I walked up the stairs of the Lee Library toward the fourth floor, which houses the marvelous Utah Valley Family History Center, I was in a reflective mood. The year 1990 had come much sooner than I had thought it would back in 1956 when I had gazed into the future after Marilyn and I came out of the temple where we had just been married.

As part of my family history effort, I planned to review again the family record that we had already sent in as part of what was known in the 1960s and 1970s as the four-generation program.

Upon entering the center, I removed my overcoat and laid it on a nearby chair. I then found and opened the drawer that contained hundreds of small white boxes in which are the film copies of the four-generation family group records. My eyes swept the labels until I saw the box that contained the D's. I removed it from the drawer, turned, and headed toward the row of microfilm readers where I could view the magnified records.

I was not prepared for the emotional experience that was about to occur. I turned the film ahead until I was reading "Durrant" records. Then, suddenly, my eyes focused on a record wherein I, George Donald Durrant, was recorded as the father. Just below my name was the name Marilyn Kay Burnham. Thinking of the joy that our marriage had brought into my life, my heart softened, but I was still not quite prepared for what I was soon to see.

I slightly lowered my gaze. On the line for the first child was the name Matthew Burnham Durrant. Unbidden, my thoughts jumped back to 1957 to Fort Chaffee, Arkansas. And to the birth of our firstborn child.

Next was the name Kathryn Kay Durrant—our first daughter. I could see her as a baby and then as a radiantly beautiful woman, and tears welled up in my eyes. Next was Devin. Instantly I pictured myself in the Cooley Memorial Hospital in Brigham City witnessing his birth. Marinda, Dwight, and Warren were the next three names. I thought of each of them, and my heart overflowed with gratitude.

What happened next was among the three or four most penetrating emotional experiences of my life. You see, no more children were listed. I looked up to the date when we had submitted this record— 1965. To myself I softly spoke, "When we compiled this record and sent it to the Church, we had only six children."

With that thought, a chill started across my

shoulder and swept down my back as I asked myself, "What if that had indeed been the final number of our children? What if we had not had Sarah and Mark join our family?" I could scarcely bear the thought. Tears flooded my eyes as I considered all that would not have been part of my life—of our lives—if we had not had Sarah and Mark.

In my mind I could see tall, beautiful Sarah, who was at that time a student at BYU. To me, she was the most beautiful student in the entire student body. The day before, she and I had walked to a devotional at the Marriott Center. As we walked along she had slipped her hand under my elbow and held my arm. I wanted to shout out to all twenty thousand who were gathering there, "Look at me, everyone! See this beautiful girl at my side? She is my daughter. I am her father, and we love each other!"

As I thought these things, I remembered there was no way to adequately describe the joy that is called Sarah.

Then my mind flew east one thousand or more miles to Kentucky. I could see there a tall missionary. It was my son—our son—Mark. I could see him plainly, and he was smiling as he walked toward another door. What seemed like a million joyous memories of all that Mark and I had experienced together crowded forward to gain my attention. "Oh," I said to myself. "What would I have ever done if I had never known and loved little Markie?" When the other family members were grown and had left home, he and I would go to football games and, joined by Marilyn, we'd go to the Sizzler restaurant. When he'd come home for dinner or later at night, he'd shout, "J'ai faim, Mère." Both Marilyn and I doubt that any child ever brought such joy to his parents. Without him, my heart's happiness and Marilyn's would have been full but not so overflowing as he had made it. I wanted to reach out across half a continent and take him in my arms and hold him closer than he could ever be held.

As I looked back at the record, I said silently but desperately, "This is not our family." For an instant I wanted to write on the film's reflected image the names *Sarah* and *Mark*. But that would do no good. So I just looked up and said, "Oh, dear God, thank you for Marilyn, Matt, Kathryn, Devin, Marinda, Dwight, Warren." And then I added with emphasis, "And Sarah and Mark—the last ones."

I removed the film from the reader, put it in its box, walked to the drawer, put the film away, put on my coat, and walked down the stairs and back into the world—the wonderful world where we live as a family. I pulled my coat up higher on my neck to protect myself from the cold, but my heart was warm because Marilyn and I had all of our children, including the last ones.

So what of birth control? Well, all I can say is that when you someday look at your family group record, don't see a blank space or two where the names of your last ones could have been listed.

Be sure, therefore, to have your first one or ones, and your middle one or ones, and . . . and I get choked up as I say this, be sure, absolutely sure, that you don't stop until you have your last one.

But how will you know? Oh, you'll know, all right. You'll know. You and your spouse and the Lord will all know.

6

Being Religious in Your Little House

Whthis at I am about to say is difficult for me to
explain, but to me it is vitally important. Please mea-
sure my thoughts against yours, and someday when
we talk, tell me what you think.

The graduate school class I was taking lasted
three hours each Wednesday evening. One such
evening, ninety minutes of the class were over. The
eleven other students and I were crowded around
the candy machine, flushing out M&M's peanut can-
dies and other delicacies. In the several weeks that
we had studied together as a class, we had learned
as much while we conversed on our candy breaks
as we did in the formal setting.

I had discovered a week or two earlier that three

or four of my classmates were not much involved with religion. One was very negative about the "Mormon" church.

This night we were joking about something that had come up in our class discussion. I felt the eyes of my disgruntled friend focus on me. When a lull came in the group conversation, he expressed something I shall never forget. With great sincerity, he said, "George, the thing I like about you is that you are religious, but you don't act like you are."

Now, I realize that some may not think he had paid me a compliment, but to me, it placed me right where I longed to be. Somehow I feel deeply that we need to *be* religious rather than to *act* religious.

Of course, if we are religious, we will act religious. But sometimes I fear that I act religious and hope that that alone will be enough.

Let me go back in time from the experience I just described and try to explain why my friend's words were registered in my soul as a compliment.

In high school I was not certain that I wanted to be religious. Whether it was real or just imagined on my part, I felt that many who were religious had a "goody-goody" attitude that didn't fit the pattern of what I wanted to be.

But in my early college years, I began to feel that what I had seen had not been religion but had instead been counterfeit religion. I had shied away from it, mistakenly thinking that it was real religion. It was then that many awakenings began in my soul. I began to wonder what my direction should be.

While in this state of mind, I walked alone to the Smith Fieldhouse and took my seat near the back. Some eight thousand BYU students were there for our weekly devotional assembly. President Ernest L. Wilkinson introduced a man I did not know nor had ever heard of before. The man then began to speak.

Somehow the words he spoke reached way back to where I was seated, and the spirit he conveyed caused the words to sink deep into my heart. He spoke of miracles, healings, the Maoris of New Zealand, and the power of the priesthood. His words were impressive, but more than words impressed me that day. I sensed that this conveyed real religion.

His words were sometimes sobering and made me wonder. But at other times, his words were humorous and caused me to chuckle and smile. From his first sentence to his final amen, I felt feelings that I had never felt before.

After the closing prayer, I wanted to go down and speak to him, but instead I slipped quickly out of the side door and hurried up the hill toward the Cougareat. As I walked, many thoughts filled my mind and joy filled my heart. Nearing the Joseph Smith Building, I said to myself, "I want to be like that man. I want to be religious, and at the same time I want to be real."

I know that Jesus Christ is the pattern, and our goal ought to be and is to be like Him. But, oh, how glad I am when someone who, like me—a struggling ordinary man—shows me a close-up pattern of how to live.

Matthew Cowley, an Apostle of the Lord, did that for me on that day so long ago, and I have never forgotten the goal that I set that day.

Religion for me is many things, but its biggest payoff is that it works. It really is the ultimate solution to problems, large or small. Religion really is happiness.

It is my belief that all, especially the disgruntled,

would, if they knew the sweetness of religion, not turn away from the church doors but would pound on those doors to get in.

Why all of this in this book? Because religion, valuable as it is to each individual, is beyond measurable value to you, your spouse, and your children as you live together in your little house.

The following fabricated episode further explores what I mean. I call this experience "Shining in Darkness."

Shining in Darkness

You and your prospective spouse have come to visit me. In my front room you say, "This sure is a lovely little house. Marilyn, your spouse, sure has decorated it well. I like the multitude of pictures of you and your children and your grandchildren that covers those two whole walls of your family room. I love the water colors you did of your old family home in American Fork that you have hanging here above the piano."

Then you'd stop and stand really still. Your eyes would focus on a small object on top of the piano. After a pause of silence, your sweetheart would softly and reverently ask, "What is this?" Before I could answer, you'd declare in awe, "It seems to glow."

I'd stand by the side of the two of you, and as we set our eyes on this sacred object, I'd say, "That is one of the sixteen stones that the Lord touched for the brother of Jared so that they would radiate light."

Then, when we were seated in a way that we

could still see the stone, I'd say, "You two are going to be married, and that stone is sort of symbolic of the light that you will need to have a joyful life together."

Let's read about the stone in the book of Ether:

> And thus the Lord caused stones to shine in darkness, to give light unto men, women, and children, that they might not cross the great waters in darkness (Ether 6:3).

The two of you are about to embark on your own private barge into the great waters of married life. Children will come, and they will depend on you to keep them safe. You will need light in your family barge, or your life will be dismal and frightening.

> And it came to pass that the Lord caused that there should be a furious wind blow upon the face of the waters, towards the promised land; and thus they were tossed upon the waves of the sea before the wind (Ether 6:5).

Life's purpose is to help us all to journey to the promised land. The Lord provides the way for us to get there—a wind to move us continually in that direction. But life also has its waves, or its ups and downs:

> And it came to pass that they were many times buried in the depths of the sea, because of the mountain waves which broke upon them, and also the great and terrible tempests which were caused by the fierceness of the wind (Ether 6:6).

You already know that life often seems to bury

us in the depths of problems, despair, and discouragement. Marriage and family life don't change that, but they often enhance it. The wind the Lord allows to blow is called "opposition in all things" (see 2 Nephi 2:11). The opposition seems to hinder us, but in reality it strengthens us, and the strength we gain is what qualifies us to enter the promised land.

Let's read on:

> And it came to pass that when they were buried in the deep . . . [and] when they were encompassed about by many waters they did cry unto the Lord, and he did bring them forth again upon the top of the waters (Ether 6:7).

So there are problems awaiting you. As a matter of fact, you should expect problems if you're on the Lord's list of those sailing to the promised land.

> And it came to pass that the wind did never cease to blow towards the promised land. . . .
> And thus they were driven forth; and no monster of the sea could break them, neither whale that could mar them; and they did have light continually, whether it was above the water or under the water. (Ether 6:8, 10.)

Sure you two will have some problems; some waves will turn you upside down, and the monsters of worldly practices will pound against your barge, or I should say against your little house. A society like ours that calls evil good and good evil will be like giant whales waiting near your door to swallow you up. But through it all you will never be in darkness, because the Lord will do for you what he did for the Jaredites. He will give you light. With the light of the Lord, you can cross any ocean, and your travels will be a journey of joy.

This ends our story. Now, of course, I don't have one of those stones. I wish I did. If you ever find one, come by my house and let me have a look at it. But you know, Marilyn and I—and you also—really do have such a stone. Our whole life is like a giant stone that the Lord has touched and made to light up. But we must always remember that the brother of Jared had to do his part to get light. He had to make the stones of molten rock. We too must do our part. Your ideas on what to do to get light will be as good as mine, but because I'm writing this chapter, I'll tell you some of the things we do.

Both Marilyn and I served as missionaries. In our mission, companions bore short testimonies to each other every day. In our early days of marriage, having vivid memories of such a practice, Marilyn and I decided to, just prior to our evening prayers, bear to each other a testimony of some aspect of our knowledge of some divine truth. That daily practice has helped give continual light to our life together.

You may not want to follow such a pattern, thinking it to be a bit too much. I understand that some things seem to fit better in one's personal religious style than do others. But in this or some other way more natural to you, we all need each day and even more often to allow our minds and hearts to dwell on the things that can only be seen through our spiritual eyes. To me, this very private experience that Marilyn and I share daily helps us to never forget the eternal hope we have for our marriage and our family and to stay as close as we can to the light of the Lord.

In our prayers together, Marilyn and I only rarely

mention my work or hers. At times we pray regarding our Church callings. Sometimes we mention financial matters and decisions. But in each prayer, without exception, our most fervent appeal is for the spiritual welfare of ourselves and our children—and now that we are grandparents, for our children's children.

All of our prayers—be they individual, or Marilyn and I together, or she and I and the children—could correctly be called "family prayers" because at the heart of each prayer is the appeal that our family members will choose the right and be guided by the light of truth.

Prayer, more than any other religious practice, helps the family and gives light to help us through the storms.

But prayer needs love to make it work. We can't simply pray our marriage to a state of bliss or our children to heaven. So we pray for the power to reason, to be patient, to not force, to love, and to maintain hope. Then, somehow in time, through each family member's own agency, we can move in a more honorable, charitable, and spiritual direction.

What I have just said about testimony and prayer are to me examples of being religious without any outward or public show. But there are other things far from the public eye that go on in the family which are supremely private and which only the family members ever see. And what each sees in the family is the main determinant of the feelings each individual in the family will have about religion.

It would take volumes to cover all that could be encouraged or discovered within the private walls of a home. But nothing could be so important as kindness, good manners, respect for one another's dignity, and listening to each other's concerns. These are all part of a family's religious life.

As I think of these things, I ask, "If I were to give myself and my family a grade on how well we do on 'real' religious matters, how would we come out?" I feel we would get an A once in a while, a B at times, a C usually, and once in a while an F. But if we are trying, and praying, and hoping, and avoiding deceit, we will get an A for effort, and somehow that illustrious grade will cause things to work out.

The family dressing up, and going to church, and having strict rules, and showing absolute obedience, and behaving admirably in public—all are virtues we long for. But if the positive things that take place privately in the home are not the highest of all priorities, then any public display will be hollow and temporary.

Somehow we must make our religion not only the source of appropriate restraint but also our doorway to day-by-day joy, fun, and security, which will make our family life our best idea of just what heaven will be.

I long to have it said, "George, you and Marilyn and your children are religious, but you don't act like it. Your prayers aren't the longest nor the most poetic. Your children seem free, yet their inward behavior indicates that they have restraint. You don't seem bent on condemning those whose views are different than your own. You seem more anxious to do than to tell. Your children seem mentally, emotionally, and spiritually healthy—and so do you. And you seem like you're always laughing and having fun."

These things are not all a reality in our lives, but

they are our ideals. Living real life in a spiritual and joyous way is the highest order of religion, and by George, that is what I want and will strive for forever.

That is why I considered the remark made by that disgruntled fellow I mentioned at the beginning of this chapter to be a compliment.

7

Having an Environment of Hope in Your Little House

I've always been a dreamer. How about you? I hope you're a dreamer too. There is a line of a song that I like that goes like this: "Every dream can come true. It can happen to you if you're young at heart." I'd change one word of that so that it would say, "Every dream can come true. It can happen to you, if you're *good* at heart."

The darkest day of my life occurred while I was serving in the army at Fort Chaffee, Arkansas. I had just finished radio school and was awaiting my assignment to another post—a post that I hoped would be somewhere in the United States or in Europe, someplace where Marilyn and our soon-to-be-born baby could be with me. Our class of twenty graduates stood casually in the appointed place to await our orders. The sergeant, with papers in hand, approached quickly and called us to attention, then later to stand at ease. He began to read the first ten names. The names he read were each assigned to Germany. The next eight were assigned to various places in the United States. Only two of us remained. He paused, and then with some seeming sympathy he said, "Private Ryles and Private Durrant, you are assigned to Korea." I had dreaded such a command as one can only dread the most awful of life's circumstances. Those orders meant that for a year and a half I would not see Marilyn and the baby. My hopes and dreams were shattered. All seemed lost. I longed for it all to be a dream, a horrible nightmare. But it wasn't. An hour later Marilyn met me at the bus stop in Fort Smith. She looked at my forlorn expression, and without my telling her she knew. We joined hands and walked the several blocks home without speaking a word.

That night in our little house in Fort Smith, Arkansas, while we lay in bed, Marilyn, with her head on my shoulder, wet my shirt with her tears. She could scarcely conceive how she could, in her loneliness, care for our baby for so long. Our love bound us together in such a manner that to be separated was more painful than having a limb torn from our bodies.

Because my departure date was two months away, I decided that there was still time to have the orders changed. In desperation, I phoned the base commander. "Please, sir," I pleaded, "I know others who want to go but who are to stay in the States. Could you not intervene and change me with one of them so that I would not have to be separated from my wife and little child!"

He kindly replied, "Private Durrant, you should

not have called me. There is a chain of command, you know." But he added compassionately, "I understand your feelings. Through the years of my service, I have at times been sent away from my family. I did not want to go. But what kind of an army would it be if none of us were willing to go where we are needed?"

I wrote to my congressman, who could not help.

Our evening, and morning, and a multitude of other silent prayers were powerful because of our pure and desperate motivation. We knew that our appeals were heard in heaven, but the answer we sought did not come. As the remaining days of our being together grew smaller in number, our despair gradually pushed aside all of our hope. During those days, our baby son Matthew was born. When he was one month old, the doctor advised us that he needed an operation for a herniated navel. This medical procedure was not serious, but it could not be scheduled until the day after my appointed departure, and that grieved me greatly.

The day before I was to leave and a few days before the baby's scheduled surgery, I called a friend with whom I had served a mission. Together, by the power of the priesthood and in the name of Jesus Christ, we blessed tiny Matthew Durrant.

As my friend anointed the baby, and as I spoke the words of the blessing, I felt a miracle was occurring. However, after we said amen, I looked at his navel and noticed that the obvious condition was the same. Again hope faded.

At Fort Lewis, I was delayed for three weeks awaiting my flight to Korea. After being there for five days, I received a letter that I sensed was of great importance. Instead of opening it immediately, I placed it in my shirt pocket, left the barracks, and walked down the road a mile or so and into a clump of pine trees. There, all alone, I opened the letter.

Dear George,

I took the baby in for the operation, but the doctor examined his condition and said, "This baby doesn't need any surgery. As you can see for yourself his navel is perfectly normal."

There was much more to the letter, but my emotions were such that for the moment I could read no more. I fell to my knees in gratitude. Then, in my mind, I heard my Heavenly Father say, "All your prayers have been heard, and this is your answer. Go to Korea, and while you are gone, I will care for your family."

My heart was flooded with hope. I could feel the words of the hymn, "All is well, all is well."

I went to Korea. Each night for more than a year of nights, I walked up on a slight hill that overlooked a pleasant valley of rice fields and picturesque homes. There on that high place, I silently prayed: "Dear Heavenly Father, you promised me you'd care for my wife and son. I just wanted to remind you."

Then, though we were thousands of miles apart, it would be as though Marilyn would join me on the hill, and we would stand there together.

That experience and others have taught Marilyn and me that the hardest flame of all to extinguish is the flame of hope. Just as it flickers and seems to gasp for life, the Lord sends a surge of fuel that causes it to flame up into a bright light, giving us new vision to watch all things work together for our good.

You could relate an experience like the one I've just written. Each of us crosses the sea of life with its challenges; we all experience dark days and some dark moments. Then, when we can scarcely see a step ahead, we look up and there, shining as a guiding star, is a ray and then a gleam and then a bright light of hope.

I recall when my oldest three children were yet small, I took them to a basketball game. At that time there was troubling international news that led to much unrest and a real threat of war. As we walked toward our car, the boys talked of the future and how someday they'd play for our favorite team. I wondered if my little ones would be able to someday play in important games or if the world by then would be too troubled to allow such activities. I looked up into the heavens, and my heart again was filled with the gentle light of hope that said, "All is well, all will be well."

Somehow hope has always found itself at the very roots of our family life. As a young married couple, we dreamed and hoped for a family. That was a far greater dream than anything we longed for professionally.

Then, when the children came, hope was the fundamental principle and the foundation of the environment in which we governed them. When they were young, we dreamed of how they would be when they were in high school, and college, and on missions, and married. In our dreams, we could see our children as being "really something." We didn't tell others about our dreams. Such feelings are not public but family matters.

These hopes of what our children could become governed our style of discipline. In moments when their behavior disappointed us, our hope prevented us from actions that could have made matters worse rather than better.

Such feelings led to the glorious and motivational principle of trust. We hoped so fervently that we came to know in some way what they would become, and so we trusted them. We didn't have a multitude of rules. Our standards were summed up by the great concept of "Our Family." We would often say, "What others do or say that is different from our standards doesn't determine what we will do because in 'Our Family' there are things we don't do and things that we do do." Often, we would praise them and thank them for governing themselves by the standards of "Our Family."

The children and we, as parents, were trusted to keep standards that would bring honor and joy to our family. And, of course, having the guiding light of the Church helped us to forever know what our family standards should be.

Somehow when disagreements arose that could cause friction and rebellion, our hope held us together. Our hope gave us the courage to allow our children some freedom, because we knew they would keep the family standards. This kept us from seeing every slight deviation from the standard as a crisis that required a heavy hand on our part lest all would be lost. This, I believe, made our home a pleasant place to be.

Now, I fear that this might all seem rather idealistic. And really it is. We, like all families, have challenges that make us wonder why we can't do better. At the same time, on the average—day in and day out—life can be pretty pleasant at home when you see a vision of the future and know that all is or will be well. In the light of that hope, needed discipline can bind you together rather than tear you apart. It can help you and your spouse sense that respect for the dignity of others—of each other and the children—is far more important than our victory over the will of another.

Because of hope, my time in Korea is now a treasured memory. The hope I had there of being reunited with Marilyn and our son and our future children was always the rock upon which was built my day-by-day happiness.

That hope helped me keep the standards that would eternally guarantee our eternal family. Hope of the future drove aside the myriad temptations that surrounded the life of a military man in a far-off land.

Finally, I was aboard a troop ship headed home. After several days on the sea, I stood on the sunny deck and could see in the distance the United States' western shore. I could hear a song playing on a nearby radio. I had never heard the words before, even though I think it was an old song made recently popular. The words were, "He's got the whole world in his hands." I didn't know at the time that the words referred to our Heavenly Father, and I thought the message was strictly for me, for I truly felt that I did indeed have the whole world in my hands. I felt the sort of hope that filled my soul so full of light that my love was for a time perfect. I knew then that the world could be held in my hands. At least, the part of the world that was dear to me—the world of my family.

And so I hope and even know that when times are a bit tough, and the challenges loom larger than our courage and strength, the Lord will send a blessing of hope. That hope will heal our wounded souls just enough to let us hear the quiet voice of the Lord whisper, "Go forward toward your dreams, and as you do, I will bless you and your family, and all will be well."

8

Family Home Evenings in Your Little House

With trembling fingers, I gripped the eight-page script I had written during the previous week. It was my best effort, but would it be good enough to satisfy the other eight members of the Family Home Evening Writing Committee?

I began to read.

The first three pages discussed how, in 1963, President Harold B. Lee had re-emphasized the need for families to have a weekly family home evening. I noticed Sister Hale, our leader, nod her approval at the direction I was taking. Grant Hardy, perhaps the most astute member of our committee, moved forward, then backward in his chair. The other six members sat motionless.

I read on, describing experiences I had heard others report regarding their family home evenings.

Soon I came to the page where I had expressed my feelings of what had happened with Marilyn and me and our children.

I was not prepared for what happened next. From the sixth page of the script, I read about asking my children if they could tell me of a personal experience of a prayer being answered. Seven-year-old Kathryn replied, "Last week when the garbage truck came, one of the garbage men had a big bandage on his hand. I prayed that his hand would get better. Today when he came, the bandage was gone."

I felt considerable emotion as I read that simple story aloud. I paused, but then I was able to carry on.

Next I read:

"We sat in our front room using the manual. The lesson we were discussing centered on saying good things about each other. One by one, each child was the target, and all the rest of us took turns saying good things about that child.

"A beautiful spirit came into the room.

"Finally, it was Marilyn's turn to be the one. Each child quickly stated something good about her. Finally it was our ten-year-old son Matt's turn to speak.

"He softly said, 'Dad, if I said all the good things that I know about Mom, we'd be here all night.'"

Having read these words, a feeling of love and gratitude came into my heart so forcefully that I could hardly continue to read.

After pausing long enough to take a deep breath, I read, "Oh, my dear son, I feel the same way about her. I love her with all my heart."

Having said this, a flood of dear feelings for my family and for the joy of family home evening came into my soul.

I could read no more. I began to gently sob.

My kind associates spoke tender words of comfort, even though my sobs had become contagious and they too were in tears.

Finally, after a minute or so, I gathered myself together and read the conclusion of the script.

The script was never used, but that didn't matter, because through writing and reading it, I had a spiritual witness that having family home evenings can result in sacred blessings that can be a major force in uniting a family forever.

I should add to the above account that I am not much of a crier. The last time I had cried like that had occurred some eleven years earlier. On that occasion, I had been a missionary in England. It was at a time while I was speaking to seven other missionaries about Joseph Smith's prayer in the grove and the answer he received. As I bore testimony that the young prophet had seen our Heavenly Father and his Son, Jesus Christ, I realized for the first time that what I was saying was true, and I wept tears of joy. And now years later, a most significant matter—the blessings of family home evening—had brought me to tears again.

It was interesting to me that just at the same time that drugs began to be more liberally available to all people, especially the young, the Lord inspired the prophet to emphasize the need for families to gather together each week for family home evening.

We followed the prophet's counsel, and it has made a profound impact on our family. I shall now try to give more detail about that impact. I wish I had written what I'm about to say some twenty years ago while our entire family was still at home, and while we were in the midst of our most exciting family home evenings. My experiences with this program were then fresh in my mind and heart. But I shall do my best to look back and to recapture my memories of this vital part of our family life.

Memories of Family Home Evenings

I wish you could have looked through the window of our little house each Monday night beginning some twenty-seven years ago. Almost without exception, on those glorious evenings you would have seen Marilyn, the children, and me gathered together for family home evening. But, of course, you wouldn't have been able to look in, because the first thing we always did on Monday night was to pull the drapes together and to close the door so that no one could see in and so that our family could be totally separated from the world, safely settled inside our little house.

Because the past is gone and the children have now scattered, I feel free to go public with something which, at the time of its happening, was so very private. So now let me pull aside the drapes and open the front door of my memories and invite you to review with me some of our family's happiest times—our family home evenings.

Scene 1: A winter's night in 1965

Having just decided to follow the counsel of the prophet, I am leading our family in one of our very first family home evenings. You can see by the rather intense expression on my face that I sense the importance of this experience. I obviously know that it is my responsibility to teach my children the gospel, and that it is serious business. As you observe, you notice that the children are a bit fidgety and aren't paying attention to my words. You note that my voice is growing louder, and my eyes are starting to glare. You hear me say, "Children, I'm getting upset at the way you are acting. Our Church leaders have told us as parents to have family home evening and to teach the gospel to our children, but you don't seem willing to listen. You sit there pushing each other, laughing and acting like you don't care. Well, I care, and I'm getting tired of your behavior. Now, if you don't start listening, you're all going to be sent to bed. I'm not kidding. I just won't put up with your nonsense. Is that clear?"

You notice that my speech has silenced the children. I soften my voice, and in quieter tones I ask, "Do you enjoy our family home evenings?"

You can read the children's minds as they think, "Oh, yeah, we enjoy sitting here having you shout at us and threaten us. We love family home evenings."

I soften further and ask, "What can we do to make our home evenings better?"

Matt, our oldest son, replies, "Next week could we have Mom teach the lesson?"

You notice I seem a bit crushed by this remark, but then you see me smile because you sense that I have received the message and know what needs to be done.

Scene 2: One week later

You notice that as I call the children together I

am smiling. I quickly pull the drapes. I head towards the big soft chair where I sit to conduct the affairs of our family home evening. You are slightly shocked to see me step away from the chair and sit on the carpet.

"Let's all sit on the floor," I suggest. Then I say to myself, "We've pulled the drapes so that no one, including the teacher development leader, can look in to make sure we are doing things right. So, being private, I feel comfortable in having my family home evening just the way we want to."

You whisper to me, "Isn't this arrangement—sitting on the floor—a bit too informal? After all, we are here to discuss the gospel."

I laugh and say, "Relax. If you can't relax, we'll have to ask you to leave."

Then I take a deep breath and say a private prayer, "Oh, dear Lord, help me to relax. Help me, no matter what happens here tonight, not to get upset. Help me to be pleasant." (After that I never got upset at a family home evening. If I felt such an emotion coming on, I would call "time out" and go get a drink of water. As I said, I never got upset again. But I did drink quite a lot of water.)

Continuing, I say, "Children, here is the family home evening manual. I'll read some lesson titles, and you tell me which one sounds the best for tonight."

Before long Matt hears one that appeals to him and makes it known.

"All right," I respond, "that will be a good one. Matt, here is the manual. Notice the pictures. While the rest of us play 'Eency Weency Spider,' you take a few minutes to read the lesson. Then you will be our teacher."

"I can't prepare in just a few minutes."

"Sure you can. You just do your best and get us started, and we'll all say what we think, and we will have a good lesson and a very good time."

You are quite impressed at how well Matt teaches. I am too.

Finally, I sense I have something in my heart that I want to say regarding a point in the lesson. I begin to speak, when little Warren starts to tumble on the carpet. I feel myself getting a bit upset, but I catch myself and call, "Oh, look at Warren tumble. He is so good at tumbling. Watch him tumble over here. Now watch him tumble back. We are sure glad our boy Warren can tumble so well. Now watch him sit up and listen to what Father says." Then I continue with my brief but heartfelt thought.

You feel a spirit of love and happiness and fun in our home. And you like what you see, but you wonder, "Is this the way it should be? Shouldn't we be sitting in chairs like we do at Church meetings? Shouldn't our lesson be more like learning the names of the ten lost tribes?"

But you don't say anything because you are enjoying things too much.

Scene 3: Springtime 1966

You've noticed that the children seem to like family home evening better all the time. You also observe that they are sometimes reluctant to come when I call. But tonight there seems to be considerable enthusiasm to begin. You wonder if that is caused by the fact that when each of them looked in the fridge, they saw a big bottle of Sprite and a large banana cream pie. As each saw this great treat, each said, "Can we have some now?" Marilyn replied, "Not yet, we are saving that for our family home evening treat."

Each child gleefully replied, "I love family home evening!"

You can hear it ringing in your ears, "I love family home evening!" Somehow you sense that a family that loves family home evening will always be a happy family.

Later, you note that while we are all eating our banana cream pie and drinking our Sprite, I am talking about how we can all do better on performing our family chores. You sense that the children feel good talking about family chores because the subject, or at least the pie—or perhaps both—taste so good.

Scenes 4 through 1400

You come back each week for many, many weeks. You notice some things are always the same. One is that I always get things started and preside. Not very formally, but you agree that for the most part I am, as the father, in charge. You notice that other than pulling the drapes and calling on people to help, speaking up about a sacred subject when the time is right, and just plain being pleasant, I don't do much except just enjoy being there with my family. You also notice that Marilyn is quite relaxed. The burden of making things work on Monday night is not on her. Somehow there is no pressure on anyone. We all just do things together. The greatest contribution each of us makes is just being there.

One week you hear little Sarah say as she looks

around at each of us, "Daddy, our whole family is here." Then I look around, and think, "Our whole family is here, and we are all whole."

You notice that sometimes we don't seem to have an objective in our lesson. But you decide that that's all right because the teacher development leader can't see through the window anyway.

You're astonished that we don't sing each time and that sometimes we sing six songs. You finally get used to the idea that we don't have any particular format. We just seem to be guided by whatever we want to do, and sometimes you sense that the Spirit seems to guide us.

But sometimes you are not too impressed. Sometimes you whisper, "You're not doing this right, you know." I get a little defensive and reply, "Well, maybe you are right. But one thing you'll have to admit is that each week we do do it."

You then wonder, "Well, maybe they are doing it right. At any rate, they are all there, and they talk. Sometimes they talk about things that aren't important, such as sports and movies. But somehow when they talk about things as a family, all things that they talk about seem important."

You are quite impressed the night we put on a college fight song record and turn it to a high volume and all of us march in single file into and through each room of our house. Then, when the music ends, we all sit close on the floor and eat cookies, and talk, and wrestle, and sing, and pray, and love each other.

You really wonder about our sanity when we put down a sheet on the floor, put the popcorn popper in the center of the sheet, take off the lid, and let the popcorn zing out wherever it will as each of us dives to get our share. You dive too, and later wonder what got into you. You were grateful that night that the drapes were closed.

Well, we could go on and on and on with scenes of all the prayers, and games, and songs, and discussions, and treats, and decisions, and plans, and dreams, and expressions of love, and hopes, and feelings. If we wrote all that happened in our little house on Monday nights, our little book would rival the *Encyclopedia Britannica* in size.

So let's leave our report of family home evening memories and return to the here and now. Of course, family home evening *alone* won't fulfill all the promises made about our family being protected, but it can be the nucleus of a whole host of family activities and love that will indeed strengthen the walls of our home, so that our little house will be a safe place.

Now back to that script that I read to the committee. As I read the script that told of my feelings about our family home evening experiences, I knew then, as I do now, that getting together each week as a family can be the heart of family life both now and eternally.

And that's why, on that occasion, I knew that what I was saying was supremely important. That is why I cried with joy.

9

Big Happiness in Your Little House

A great Church leader once told me that when it comes time for him to create an earth, he is going to make watermelons the size of strawberries and strawberries the size of watermelons. Would you do that? What sort of plans do you have?

It will be exciting to someday create a world. But we don't really need to wait. We can now, in one sense, create our own world within the bigger world. As a matter of fact, my fondest dream is to each day create a world of happiness as big as the earth and a world of sorrow as small as a grain of sand.

That is why when I counsel or teach college students, I often encourage them to be teachers. Why teachers? Well, it's because good teachers are almost always happy people and because teachers, next to parents, can do more to create worlds of happiness than can any other people in any other profession.

I realize that I have just made a bold statement, and if you were to challenge me to prove it, I might be hard pressed to do so. But I will always believe its truth.

I suppose if I were not a teacher but were a doctor instead, I might do all I could to get young people to consider practicing medicine. Or, if I were a carpenter, I might extol the virtues of mastering pounding nails, ripping saws through soft pine, and molding material into a beautiful cabinet or home.

But I'm a teacher, and so I'll often raise my voice and say, "Young folks, as you consider a profession, be sure to carefully consider teaching. I'm not talking to all of you but only to you who know in your hearts that you would like to be teachers. If you are one of those, then why don't you follow your inward feelings?"

Many reply, "I'd like to teach, but I wouldn't make enough money."

To which I reply with a very long answer (almost all the remainder of this chapter is made up of my answer). Here is that answer.

Money! Don't let money or the lack of it be the primary influence on what you do for a living. Do something you love, or at least like, and if the money is plentiful—good. If the money is sparse— also good.

Let's look at the sparse money life-style. I'd write on the plentiful money life-style, but I just haven't had any experience with that. So I will stay in my area of expertise.

The best way to raise children is to have very little money. Then when they ask for things you can say no. No is a wonderful answer. It is the soil in which personal ambition and discipline best grow.

After saying no to your fourteen-year-old son's request for a four-wheel-drive mountain vehicle, you must explain why you said no. You could say, "Well, son, we just can't afford it." Soon he would resent the fact that you don't seem able to provide for your family. So instead of pleading poverty, you could say, "Let me get a pen. I want to make a note that my son wants a four-wheeler." Then say, "I'll tell you that if any young man ever deserved a four-wheeler, it is you. You are the finest son a father could ever have. And one of these days my ship will come in, and the first thing I will do is get you a four-wheeler. Maybe even a five-wheeler, because you really deserve it."

He'll probably shake his head and depart. But he'll feel good. At least sort of good, and that's good enough.

I guess what I'm saying is that not too much money plus a sense of humor and a positive outlook is a fine launching pad for a young person to head toward outer life.

Of course, a young man can't be a teacher or be in any other profession that doesn't pay much money unless he marries the right girl. A spouse who is obsessed with having more than the income allows can keep heaven out of the home and can introduce something quite the opposite of heaven.

So talk it over. Can you and your spouse learn to like hamburger cooked in forty-seven different dishes? Can you enjoy a night out at McDonald's as much as the Skyroom at the Hotel Exquisite?

One Sunday afternoon while Marilyn and I were walking home from our Sunday meetings, I said to her, "Could we have scones this evening?"

She replied, "Oh, George, scones are so much work."

"That's right," I answered. "Today in church I was thinking of the making of scones and how it fits into the law of Moses. I think that perhaps fried manna would be just like scones. I also considered that all the labor that goes into scones just barely comes within the boundaries of the amount of work that the law of Moses would allow on the Sabbath."

Marilyn seemed, at least I thought she seemed, quite impressed with my ability to relate the scriptures to life. She replied, "Well, maybe if all of the family members help, we can do it."

I was elated.

At home we all busied ourselves in the necessary tasks. One child fried eggs without turning them over. Others set the table. Marilyn cooked the scones. As usual, I served as supervisor because I feel my children should understand the role of supervisor. As I sat watching, I was happy. I was in my little house with my spouse and my children. Soon we would have scones, and we would eat them as a family. Such a scene of me and my spouse and our children getting ready to eat scones in our little house could go in the encyclopedia under the word *happiness* and also the word *joy.*

The ten of us at our round table were in heaven. We aren't rich, but I did notice that we had enough wealth that each of us had a different-colored drinking glass. Speaking of drinking, we were also going to have real milk that night. During our early married years, we often had powdered milk to drink. Well, we didn't drink much of it, but we put it in our pancakes. Real milk was quite a luxury for us. We kept it in the fridge so that it stayed so cold it was nearly frozen.

The eggs were there on a platter staring at us. The milk was ready to be poured. And the scones, a big tin bowl full, were sending up steam signals that said, "Celestial food."

Now it was time for prayer. I determined to call on one of our children who was known for giving short prayers. To do so I announced, "We will now have our prayer. Tonight let's have our smart child, the one with the good looks, the one with the great personality, give the prayer."

By now almost each child had learned to respond to this familiar setup with, "Ah, Dad, I gave the prayer last time." Then I'd call on one, and all would say, "It didn't sound like you were talking about him to me."

After prayer, we commenced eating. I said to Marilyn, "Please pass me the margarine."

She responded, "Call it butter."

But I was too honest to do that. Yet, when you put margarine on hot scones, I'm sure it thinks it's butter.

We'd each eat part of a scone and then have a slug of cold milk. I told a few funny stories, and the children booed them, even though I could tell they· wanted to burst out in uncontrollable laughter.

For dessert, we put some honey on the scones. That is really living. Happiness filled the room from top to bottom and side to side. It was as if we could hear pounding on the window, and we sensed it was just more blessings trying to come into a room already crowded full of blessings.

You don't need much money to make scones. And you don't need a formal dining room in which to eat them. All you need is a little house, one that you can afford to live in, and a spouse, and a child or ten, and a lot of love and gratitude. And if you've got all of that, you don't need much else.

You don't need things like boats and that. It's better to have a neighbor who has a boat than to have a boat yourself. Then if you're a friendly family, your neighbor will say, "Come go in my boat. When your family comes with mine, we all have a better time."

Of course, you need enough money to pay for heat and lights and basic transportation and food and dental care and on and on. Those are just the realities. But most of us could be rich on our income if we truly decided that happiness is not to be found in the prestige or the comfort of things, or elaborate travel, or entertainment. Happiness is found in the simple things like being home and eating scones and trying to make room for some stray blessings that are searching through the neighborhood looking for a family who will take them in and give them a home.

So, young friends, be a teacher or a carpenter or a lawyer or whatever you feel in your heart will help you make a world where happiness is growing ever larger and sadness is constantly shrinking. Go for that, and you'll be rich on any income.

Note: Here is Marilyn's recipe for scones!

Marilyn's Scones

In a large bowl I put:

3 cups warm water
$^1/_4$ cup sugar
1 Tbls. yeast

I let the yeast grow for 15 minutes, then add:

$^1/_3$ cup shortening
2 tsp. salt

Now I begin adding flour, one cup at a time and stirring each time. If the dough is still very sticky, I gradually add more flour until it holds together. I dump the dough out onto a floured countertop and begin to knead it. As I am kneading, I add just enough flour to keep it from being sticky. (Kneading is done by folding the dough toward me and pressing it down with the heel of my hand.) I turn it slightly and knead it again. I do this over and over until the dough is smooth and soft, but not sticky—about 15 minutes. I then roll it out onto a lightly floured countertop until it is just over $^1/_4$ inch thick. I cut it with a pizza cutter (which won't pull through the dough like a knife would) into $3^1/_2$ x 4 inch squares. Before carefully placing the scones in the hot oil, I stretch them slightly. Then I fry them, one or two at a time, in oil that is deep enough to allow them to float as they cook. When first putting them in, I poke them under the oil again and again, but I don't hold them under. This allows them to expand and puff up so they are hollow inside. The pan I use is a deep saucepan that is 5 inches deep and 6 inches across. Deep fat fryers are okay, but they require more oil and take longer to heat up. The oil will bubble up as the scones are placed in, so allow for this in the amount of oil used and the depth of the pan used. You may want to also try this with your own good bread recipe.

10

Seeing Heaven out of the Windows of Your Little House

There is nothing like an art show to motivate an artist to paint more. Or a sports event to encourage a young athlete to practice harder.

And then there is the plight of a young couple living on a meager salary going from house to house in a local Parade of Homes show. They view each new home and the elegant furniture it contains. Then, as they walk on the lush carpets and look at the luxurious draperies, all sorts of unaffordable ideas flash into their heads.

So it was with Marilyn and me. We had seen such a home show, and now, a few days later, we stood in a furniture store to see if we could make our little house look a bit more like those in the show.

As we gazed upon an Early American couch (our

favorite style then), a salesman silently approached and stood at our side. We were looking so longingly at the tweed fabric of the cushions and the mahogany wood of the arms that we hadn't noticed him until he softly spoke, "Do you folks have a house?"

"Yes, we do," I replied.

"Would that couch look good in your front room?" he asked.

"Yes, it would," Marilyn answered.

"Do you by chance have a fireplace?"

"Yes, we do," I responded.

"That Early American couch would look good by your fireplace, wouldn't it?"

"Oh, yes, it would," we both said in unison.

Then walking closer to the couch, he reached down and gently stroked one of its cushions. As he did this, he asked, "Should we deliver it on Wednesday?"

We both took a deep breath as we envisioned ourselves sitting on the couch by a fire in our little house. At that precise second, my mind returned to the reality of the situation. Timidly and with deep regret registering in my voice, I stated, "But we don't have any money."

He stroked the glistening mahogany arm, smiled, and asked, "What does that have to do with it?"

Encouraged, Marilyn asked, "What do you mean?"

"Well," he said as he sat down on the couch smiling, "this is comfortable." He then added, "You won't have to make a payment until next September, and the payments are very small each month."

As you can well imagine, we were greatly enticed. We stood silently, but we both leaned a bit forward toward our dream. Suddenly and miraculously, an idea crashed through the rooftop of the furniture store and landed in each of our heads. It was a revelation that came straight from the Lord. Without speaking, we followed our inspiration: we turned and ran—well, we just walked fast—out of the store and into the parking lot.

In three minutes we were in our 1952 Chevrolet. We pulled out of the crowded parking lot and were soon on the highway that let through North Ogden. On this journey, our car seemed to run more smoothly—we often had to pray as we rode just to keep the motor and transmission working together. But tonight, it fairly flew along at nearly fifty miles an hour. It was as if the Lord was blessing us because we had followed the impression he had given us. A bit later we passed Smith and Edwards's army surplus store, and then the orchards of Willard and Perry. Forty minutes later we pulled in the driveway of our house in Brigham City.

As we entered our front room and switched on our light, we each placed our coats in the closet. Marilyn and I stood close together and smiled at each other as we considered that we wouldn't have a new Early American couch. But we also didn't have another bill to pay. We already had a number of "small" monthly payments which, when added together, was almost a larger amount than our income could bear. We felt the kind of happiness that can only come to those who exercise wise constraint.

The next week, we returned to Ogden and its finest business establishment—the Deseret Industries store. There we found an Early American couch that was far more Early American than the one we'd seen before. It was so Early American that one of its arms was missing, and its cushions were worn and holey. We purchased it with the same amount of money that would have been required to make one of the forty payments the other couch would have cost.

A few weeks later, the cushions had been recovered as a project Marilyn had undertaken in a community education upholstering class. A kind woodworking teacher had fashioned us a new wooden arm that was a perfect match for the surviving one.

Even now, after more than thirty years, as I think of sitting on that couch by the fire in our little house, my heart fills with gratitude. That piece of furniture to us is a memory symbolic of all that we have learned about thrifty ideas coming in revelations to those who pay tithing.

Paying tithing doesn't solve all family financial problems, but it makes it so that with some worry, a bit of wisdom, considerable restraint, and much prayer, money matters somehow work out.

With my work, I haven't made a great deal of money, and with Marilyn working at home caring for the family, her salary was not a liberal amount. Often we have thought, "We can't make it this month," but we always did.

The children didn't have as much as we longed to give them. The necessities alone for each, when added together, came to what appeared to be more than we were making. Our appliances and cars were not always blessed by our tithing faithfulness and often broke down at times when our economy was already stretched close to the breaking point.

Now! Thinking about the details of those harrowing times makes me shake my head in disbelief that we are not in debtors prison. But all those hard times—and we realize that others have had much worse times than we have had—have made Marilyn and me fall more and more in love with each other and with the Lord. He has indeed made it so that on a clear day or night, looking out of our windows we can see all the way to heaven. And as we look, we can see our Heavenly Father looking out at us. We can see him open the windows of heaven and pour out so many blessings that we scarcely have enough room to contain them.

11

Kidding Around in Your Little House

After my teaching day is done, I walk down the hill past the Smith Fieldhouse. My heart feels the sort of pure happiness that is so often the lot of someone who loves his work. Soon I cross University Avenue and walk the final three blocks home. My pace quickens as I turn the last corner and have just over one hundred yards to go. My heart pounds with excitement as, in my mind, I already can see Marilyn standing with her nose pressed against the window, looking out to catch the first glimpse of her handsome, homecoming husband.

Now, if you know Marilyn, you are already laughing at what I just wrote. And when Marilyn reads the above, she will in jest agree, "Oh yeah, I can hardly do anything all day long except wait for him to return."

Somehow my semi-sincere statements and Marilyn's gentle counterattacks are the spice that makes me look forward each night to coming home. The children are all married now, except Mark, and he is on a mission. Whereas for years I came home to a throng of excited children, now I come home to just Marilyn. Why is it that coming home is even sweeter now than ever before?

There are, of course, many reasons. But one important one is that Marilyn and I like to kid around and have fun. Now, don't get me wrong. Often I am far too sober when we are together, but sometimes I wish you could see me. I come home and I'm really funny. Well, at least sort of funny. And when I am, Marilyn is funny back, and when we are funny like that we sense and often say things that let us know that we are deeply in love.

I don't know what it is about kidding around and laughing that makes it so much easier to have love flare up in your heart. But it seems to me that having fun without having to do fun things creates a feeling that is to love what rich fertile soil is to a tender plant.

I wish sometimes I was funnier and that Marilyn was too. Often we don't seem to be in a fun mood, and so we just sit and act like duds—at least I do.

Maybe that's all right; maybe much of life is best lived as a dud. But I'm sure glad that quite often we rise up and have some homemade kidding around.

Here is an example of some pure fun. We've had dinner and Marilyn is about to leave for her calligraphy class. (To me, she is the best calligrapher in Utah and even up as far as Idaho.) I gently say, "Marilyn, don't be goofing off in your calligraphy class. You are not there to have fun—but to work."

She quickly replies, "Working is fun when you're

a calligrapher." Then, because I'm a water colorist, she says, "It's you water color people who never have any fun."

I reply, "That is because water color is tough to do. It's not easy like calligraphy."

By then she's out of the door, and I'm chuckling to myself about my victory. As I press my nose against the window and watch her go, I say to myself, "I miss her already, and she isn't even out of the driveway."

I called the above "victory," but it has been some thirty plus years since I won or even desired to win a battle of wits with Marilyn. She always wins, but I constantly award myself the sportsmanship trophy because I am so goodnatured about my losses to her. And when she makes her supposedly funny remarks, I don't ever laugh, because that would cause her to think that she is clever. Sometimes, however, I find myself thinking, "She really is funny." Then I realize again that the way she says funny things about me makes me know how much she adores me.

I recall a conversation we had after I returned from my mission. I was telling her a rather serious story of some of my high school frustrations— things such as my not being a star athlete, or popular, or a student-body leader. Suddenly she was holding her left hand in front of her with her thumb and forefinger about two inches apart. At the same time she was moving her right hand back and forth near the left hand. Simultaneously she was humming a rather high pitch. I stopped and said, "What are you doing?"

She replied, "I'm playing the world's smallest violin to accompany the world's saddest story."

I felt like bursting out in laughter, but all I could

do was say, "Very funny." I grabbed her hand and said, "You'd never get away with such antics if I didn't love you so much." And, oh, how I did and still do love such futile efforts on her part to be funny!

People who know both Marilyn and me think I'm funny and Marilyn is sober. Not so. Within the walls of our home and our love, she is the funny one. And as I write that, I chuckle to myself and feel so grateful to have a funny wife—a funny friend.

I could go on and on about her humor, but she'd read it and become prideful. So I'll leave it there for now.

In our home through the years, my children, who can't seem to tell a quality sense of humor from an average one, have chosen to use their laughs more frequently in support of their mother's remarks than mine.

When she tells them of my inability to dance, they laugh. Of course, that makes me feel bad. I tried to learn to dance in high school, but in those days you danced really close to the girl and that was too much for me. I took a social dance class in college and finally got an E. But I was better than that. It's just that I could never seem to get the beat.

Once, when Marilyn broke her foot, I thought I'd turn the tables on her, so one night, in front of the children, I said, "Marilyn, I've been thinking I'd like to go dancing. Should we go tonight?" I felt quite clever in my remarks, but she replied, "I don't want to have you break my other foot."

The children, who couldn't see the humor in my remarks, roared with laughter at hers, and all that did was encourage her and make her laugh at her own supposed joke. Inside, I was beside myself with the happy feelings of such fun. But I just protested,

"Way to go, children, laugh all you want. But just remember you are laughing at someone who loves you more than can ever be said." They looked at me, and Marilyn did too, with that wonderful look of complete love.

It's as I said earlier. Growing right out of the soil of kidding around come feelings of love that somehow in such moments can be expressed with surprising power.

Marilyn and the children enjoy kidding me about my home town—American Fork, Utah. Whenever we go through there, I ask for a moment of silence. Never have they granted my request. Each time, led by Marilyn, they say things like, "Your graduating class *would* have gone in every direction, but there weren't enough graduates to go all four directions." They laugh, and if it's dark enough in the car so they can't see me, I smile. Then I say, "I wish we lived here because I'd love to see you play ball and do other things for American Fork High School." Then I sing the school song. "Dear old A. F. High; yes, we will love you till we die." They soon join in the singing because they know the words, but they don't sing it with the dignity it deserves.

You fathers might be saying, "I think it would be fun to kid around like that, but I don't like to lose my dignity as a father. Besides, we are more of a loving family, and we don't like to tease each other at all."

I agree, but I can't live up to what you say, so we go on goofing off. I think you also could do a little more of that. I know that in our family we don't do as much as I'm making it appear. But once in a while, and I wish more often than that, we have a ball, and it never costs us a penny. It all happens when we least expect it—eating, riding along, at family home evening, getting ready for prayer, at bedtime, after a ball game. It isn't something that can be planned. It has to just happen. But it will happen if you'll let it and even encourage it. And Dad is often the best one to be at the receiving end of the loving gibes.

I recall recently reading a student's paper on life in his family. His father was raised in a small southern Utah town. The family now lives in California. They often make fun of his small-town heritage. On family trips to Utah, he brags all the way across the desert about his town and his exploits as a boy. The family always turns off the freeway and drives up and down the streets of his town. Looking on every corner, they semi-sarcastically say, "I can't see it, Dad—is the statue they built of you on that corner or the one over there? Where is it, Dad? As great as you tell us you were, the statue must be here somewhere. Where is it, Dad?" The dad replies, "It's here somewhere. Someday we will find it."

As I read that story, I longed to be in the car to see that beautiful mother say, "Well, Harold, it looks like it's not built yet." Then all the children would laugh, and I would sense the family feeling a closeness to Dad and each other.

Yes, there's much to be said for kidding around, for the gentle, good-taste teasing of someone who likes to feel the love of being teased.

Such teasing can also extend into the workplace. One of my faculty friends calls me "the handsome George Durrant."

I reply, "Brent, your words are redundant. You're saying the same thing twice."

He chuckles and answers, "When I say 'the handsome George Durrant,' it is not redundant. It is an oxymoron."

I don't know what that word means, but as we

chuckle together, I find myself loving him all the more.

So what does it all mean? I don't know. But I do know that in our family we sometimes kid around, but more often we are pretty serious because life is pretty serious. But when we kid around and sort of feel lighthearted, we can often more easily say, "I love you." And when that is said, life, even though sometimes difficult, seems to go along much better.

12

The Unseen Room That Is Part of Your Little House

Have you ever wondered just where the most beautiful spot on the earth is located? You need not wonder any longer, for I have located that spot.

If you will drive to my home town, American Fork, you will not yet have found the most beautiful place, even though you might think you have. Even though you are not yet at the most beautiful spot, you are close.

Turn north at the American Fork Tabernacle and proceed some five miles up that road. There you will find the small community called Alpine. It is a beautiful place, but you aren't yet in that most beautiful spot. Pull up to the local grocery store across the street from the city park. Roll down your car window and ask a passerby, "Where is the cemetery?"

After you've received directions, drive the few blocks to the cemetery. Now you are nearly there, but not quite. Drive in the entrance and go straight ahead. You'll see a road going up a hill. Proceed up that road to the top of the hill, park near the evergreen trees, and get out of your car. Walk about thirty paces north.

Now look to the south, and you'll see a valley and a plain leading several miles to Utah Lake. Then look north to the lower plains that soon slope up to some rugged, inspiring cliffs. Look east and west to the valley floor and then to the higher hills.

Then say to yourself, "Yes, George is right. This does appear to be the world's most beautiful spot, for in every direction I see beauty unsurpassed."

Why did I send you to such a place? Well, it is because that is where I desire to build my millennial home. I stood there once with my son Matt. Matt is in the legal profession. I said to him, "Matt, why don't you draw up some legal documents that will someday make this property available to me so that I can build my terrestrial house here."

He replied, "But, Father, this is a cemetery. There are graves all around on this hilltop. You can't build here."

"Son," I replied, "these people buried here are pioneers who settled Alpine. Surely in the morning of the first resurrection they will arise and depart. Thus, this hilltop, which is the world's most beautiful spot, will be a vacant lot. And it is then that I'll start to build."

Matt listened, but even though several years have passed, I don't think he has done a thing about my request.

And now that you know about the spot, you'll probably rush in at the beginning of the Millennium and build a condominium while I'm down at the city hall trying to get a building permit.

So I'm not really counting on that property or that home. Instead, when the Millennium begins, I think I'll just build a room on my present house and live there; after all, I've been told that heaven is just an extension of a happy home.

As a matter of fact, we already sort of have an extra unseen room on our house, or at least on our home. It's a special place where our family members go when they die and get to leave us for a little while.

Marilyn's mother, Bea, died on New Year's Day. She's sort of there living in the other room while she goes forth doing all that she now does.

We miss her. The other day my little two-year-old granddaughter, Eliza, said to her mother, "I want Grandma 'Bee' to come back." Someday little Eliza's wish will come true, and all those who were part of our family will come home to live with us again.

My fondest dream since Marilyn and I established our little house was to live long enough to see all of my children reared. Now that that has come about, I'd like to live long enough to see my grandchildren reared. Then, if I could, I'd like to live long enough to see my great-grandchildren reared, and then. . . .

But there will come a time when I will need to move from our seen to our unseen room. Perhaps the unseen room is really the "family room." There, in that room, I shall join my parents and their parents and theirs. Then finally Marilyn and the children, and someday their children, will all come to live in our heavenly family home.

Life is indeed eternal. In most ways that really count, there is no death.

This knowledge of our eternal destiny is a bright light and a constant direction for our family. Separation at death is difficult, but it is sweet when we look forward to a grand reunion that will someday bring us all together again.

13

Face Your Little House Toward the Temple

The wind whistled across the frozen snow of the Korean hillside. I was alone near the outer fence of a one-half square mile army compound. I carried my M-1 rifle over my shoulder.

I felt little threat from enemy because the war had ended two years earlier. But I still felt lonely and knew that the cease-fire treaty was shaky and that trouble could come my way.

On that night, I felt a pang of pain as I thought of Marilyn and little, newborn Matthew, who were so many miles away. Thinking of home caused me to reflect on all that I held dear.

Prompted by those tender thoughts of family and home, I began to softly sing "Come, Come, Ye Saints." I sang all the verses I could remember. Then

I began to sing "O My Father." Unspeakable joy filled my heart as I sang.

Soon I said in a low voice, "I'm here now in this beautiful land so far from my family." Then I smiled broadly as I exclaimed, "But pretty soon I'll be going home!"

On another night in Korea, I had a most sacred experience. (I speak of Korea because it was the only time I've been away from my little house and my family for more than a few days since Marilyn and I were married.) I had tried out for and had made the group basketball team. The dressing facilities for my teammates and me were not at all private. This bothered me because I wore my temple garments. I wore them all during my army experience because I had promised the Lord I would do so and because they made me always feel so much at home.

As we undressed to put on our basketball uniforms, I tried desperately to be as discreet as possible. But my teammates noticed, and sometimes laughingly and always curiously would ask, "What are those?"

I would smile, for I knew they didn't mean any disrespect. I knew they didn't know. I would answer by saying, "Sometime I'll tell you more about what they are."

One night we were all retiring in our small basketball team barracks. One of the fellows said, as he saw me go to my upper bunk, "George, you told us you'd tell us about your underwear."

I sensed that the time was right. I asked all twelve of my teammates to listen carefully, and they did.

"My friends," I said, "these underwear are called temple garments, and they are sacred. I'll tell you why.

"When I met Marilyn, my wife, I fell deeply in love. I asked her to marry me, and she agreed. Our marriage ceremony was in the Salt Lake Temple."

I asked, "Have you all seen the Salt Lake Temple or any other Mormon temples?" All acknowledged that they had seen a temple. Each remembered the beauty of the temple.

I continued, "Outwardly the temples are beautiful. But inside their beauty is heavenly." And then I said, "It was inside the temple in the most holy room where Marilyn and I were married.

"There in the temple we made serious promises to God, our Heavenly Father. We promised we'd do all we could to show our love to him and to each other. In return, he promised us that if we kept our covenants that we made with him, he would bless us so that we would be together forever.

"Part of what we did as we made those sacred covenants and received the promises of the Lord was to begin to wear these sacred garments. We strive, as I have here, to keep them from being seen by others, but they are always known to me. And they constantly remind me that if Marilyn and I keep our promises, we will indeed be together, not until either of us dies, but forever."

I paused, and there was a long silence.

Now, of course I'm not able to remember perfectly each word that I said. But I believe the foregoing account to be accurate in its general content. What I remember most vividly was saying, "You men know how much I treasure letters and pictures from home. Being separated from Marilyn and little Matt is the most difficult thing I've ever endured. I long to return home and to never again be separated from my family. These underwear, these garments, constantly remind me of Heavenly Father's commandments and my promises to obey them. But more than that, they remind me that my family can be together eternally."

I said no more. Nor did they. The sweet Spirit of the Lord filled the quiet room.

In the weeks that followed, my teammates understood. I continued in my corner of the dressing room to dress so that no one would see, but sometimes the opposing team who dressed with us would see, and in an amused tone, they would ask, "What are those?"

My teammates would quickly answer, "Those are part of his religion. They are sacred." The other players would reply, "Oh," and the matter would end.

When King Benjamin was to give his historic and profound talk, the people came together at the temple to await his words. The text says: "And they pitched their tents round about the temple, every man having his tent with the door thereof towards the temple" (Mosiah 2:6).

I feel it is significant that each family's door faced the temple. With that in mind, I advise young people, "When you build your little house for you and your spouse, face it toward the temple."

They look at me as if to ask, "Are you serious?"

I reply, "Oh, I know you can't always physically face your house toward the temple, but spiritually you can."

Be sure that you and your spouse and your children always face your lives toward the temple, and as you do you'll always know where you stand, and you'll always stand on sacred ground.

Yes, the hill in Alpine is indeed a beautiful spot. But the most beautiful spot on the earth can be the spot wherever you build your family home in this life and in the next. It is my wish for our family and yours that you can make it the most beautiful of all places by choosing to marry someone who desires to face toward the temple, someone you love spiritually, physically, and in every other way. And when you have found that certain someone, and that certain someone has found you, invite the Lord to touch the two of you and make you light up to be happiest of all families. Invite children to come into your little house and love and be loved by them. Within the walls of your house, be privately and deeply religious, first by deed and also by word. Let hope and vision undergird your family government and discipline. Let family home evenings be the center of a host of pleasant family experiences. Live on your income, and thus ensure that your happiness will always be far larger than the space between your walls. Pay tithing so that you'll be able to look out of your window and see the windows of heaven as the blessings come from above.

Between your serious moments, be sure to kid around and express love. Always remember the room where grandparents have gone and where we will go, and where our children and grandchildren will come to be with us. It is the place where we will all be together forever.

But a room is too small for all the hope and love and family we will have in heaven. Surely to meet our celestial needs we will need more than a room or even a little house; we will need a mansion.

Maybe that is what the Lord had in mind when he said, "In my father's house are many mansions. . . . I go to prepare a place for you." (John 14:2.)

Marilyn has read the manuscript for this book up to this point, but now, without her knowledge, I'd like to add a personal note:

Why don't you and your family come over to our

happy mansion in heaven sometime. We'll have a family home evening and talk about good things. Then we'll have a huge pan of scones. Don't call first, because Marilyn might answer. Just come.

With love,
George D.